750

Theseourmothers

The Sea Our Mother

Sea (S)mothers

(S)our Mothers

The S e our mothers

Or: The Disintegrating Chapter

by Nicole Brossard
translated by Barbara Godard

Coach House Quebec Translations

These Our Mothers was first published as
L'amèr ou le Chapitre effrité in 1977 by
Les Editions Quinze, Montreal.

Coach House Quebec Translations are edited by
Barbara Godard and Frank Davey.

The translation and publication of this
edition have been assisted by grants from
the Canada Council and the Ontario Arts Council.

This translation was edited by Ray Ellenwood.

Also in translation by Nicole Brossard:

A Book (Un livre), 1976, translated by Larry Shouldice
Turn of a Pang (Sold-out), 1976, translated by
    Patricia Claxton
Daydream Mechanics (Mécanique jongleuse), 1980,
    translated by Larry Shouldice

CANADIAN CATALOGUING IN PUBLICATION

Brossard, Nicole, 1943 –
    [L'amèr, ou, Le chapitre effrité. English]
    These our mothers, or, The disintegrating chapter

(Coach House Quebec translations)
Translation of: L'amèr, ou, Le chapitre effrité.
Poems.
ISBN 0-88910-260-0

I. Title. II. Title: The disintegrating chapter.
III. Title: L'amèr, ou, Le chapitre effrité. English. IV. Series.

PS8503.R62A4313   C841'.54   C83-098557-3
PQ3919.2.B76A4313

Preface

Prefaces should not be apologies. Most of the games Nicole Brossard plays with her readers are accessible to anglophones. In opening them up for active readerly participation, I have made greater use of graphic modes for presenting double meaning than she has, but I have followed examples in the original text.

One game defies translation however, one with the rules of grammar which is fundamental to the understanding of *L'amèr*, notably the question of gender agreements in French which has no equivalent in English with its neutral pronouns. I have transferred this play to the word his-tory / her-story more familiar to anglophone feminists. The question of the silent 'e' at the end of words, voiced only in song or poetry where it is termed 'feminine rhyme', has been more difficult to resolve. In several cases Brossard removes the 'e' from the end of a word as in *laboratoir* (p. 35) to mark the absence of the feminine in the activities carried out there. At other times, as in the title *L'amèr* the silent 'e' is removed from *mère* (mother) to underline the process of articulating this silence, of moving toward a neutral grammar, which occurs in the text.

Alert readers will catch the many allusions in the text, terms like 'difference' and 'erasure' leading back to Derrida, while 'deployment', 'intensity', 'repetition' evoke fellow deconstructionist, Gilles Deleuze.

May the intensity of your involvement as reader be as great as mine and you extend its creation in new directions to make this the text of bliss it works to be.

BARBARA GODARD

and the mother contracts at a distance ...
HUGUETTE GAULIN

It's combat. The book. Fiction begins suspended mobile between words and the body's likeness to this *our* devouring and devoured mother

Fictive theory: words were used only in the ultimate embrace. The first word lips and sticky saliva on her breasts. Theory begins there when the breast or the child moves away. Strategic wound or suspended meaning.

The **S**e our mothers

I killed the womb. *My* life in summer the moon. *My* death. Thirty years separate me from life, thirty from death. My mother, my daughter. Mamma, Mam*elle*, Mamilla, a single life, mine. Clandestine system of reproduction. Anonymous matrix and matter.

the same day. One black sex, one white sex. One I caress, the other I wash. Cyprine juices, urine. Orgasm and labour as two sides of the same entity. Your bodies, lesbian lover and daughter. I write so I won't engulf and hurt your bodies and so as to find in them my void, my centre.

War measures. Interned by the matrix. The body of ... like a missing link, found again in the water. Their industry of fantasies made her lose her sense of reality. The body of ... rots. He retrieves the phantasm for his own ends. Recycled body.

another day. The alphabet. In the beginning. Desire brings me endlessly back to it and, my present ... forward flight. What happens to a woman who recognizes this process and encounters its inexorability in fact, in age and in *his*tory, in body.

Each whirlpool had one facet. Each flake its geometry. One figure mine, one other, also different from you, another woman. Unspoken. Three-faced incest that refuses the lie yet whose eye nonetheless keeps all traces of it. The origin of Ah! From the depths of the throat. Chaos, our limbs afire. Maybe to burn out the fuse before the letter. To set our breasts ablaze. Sour milk. And the mamilla dyed green as in science fiction. Because the trial has begun. At last two generations of women have touched each other on the mouth and the sex and found their target. Each whirlpool with a different woman, because I had to go into black, water, blue and drown the acidity of white.

Cramp clutching the belly and clutching a male who cannot go in. Now none may enter the laboratory unless he is transformable. I have killed the womb and exploded the S^{ea}_{our} mother. Below the horizon in there alchemy, a prose of negotiation, is practised. As though to proliferate cells of desire when fascination ferments its violence. Great voracious fiction.

My mother is drinking her beer. I don't know what she expects from me. What could I expect from her, if not from myself. The sisterhood of women is the ultimate test of human solidarity laying itself open to another beginning of delusions of grandeur.

My mother is drinking her beer. She is writing while I wait for her to give me a cookie.

It's between her legs, sliding always a little more painfully for her, for me. A spurt of white. Panic. Between life and death. Blue funk.

she has breasts, pubic hair. Me pink. Her body, her texture makes my blood turn. She whispers. Her daughter-mother's lips. Shifty weather makes us die between two waters. A big white monkey puts his arms about her. I have split her soul in two: girl's sex. Humanity passes over us like a (c)rushing roller. Big neurotic primate. Gross anal. His-tory.

With a different woman, when we used to drink a lot, we didn't make love. We used to write, sitting facing each other. State of emergency. Don't let the battle break out between our bodies. Let the connection happen somewhere else. So that our bodies won't be mutilated immediately by the clasp of hands, by the warm embrace. No longer impressing each other mutually. Anarchy of the couple. Narrative cut around a/s motherly dependence. System of exchange and very precise code. We can support only one body at a time. Each her own. Let's make it clear.

there is always one body too many in one's life. Each mother. Each child. The same body.

If it weren't lesbian, this text would make no sense at all. Matrix, matter and production, all at once. In relation to. It constitutes the only plausible system to get me out of the belly of my patriarchal mother. And of distancing my eye from her enough so as to see her in a different way, not fragmented into her metaphoric parts. Crossing through the symbol while I am writing. An exercise in deconditioning that leads me to acknowledge my own legitimacy. The means by which every woman tries to exist: to be illegitimate no more.

Legality for a woman: not to be born from the womb of woman. That is what ruins them both. The womb of the species. Which is reproduced from generation to generation. Bitch and bastard. Equally illegitimate. Just look at the base of the cliff. The bloody sheet or the madwoman confronting the husband-psychiatrist couple who are putting their seals on her.

Between my mother and my daughter. Lesbian rather than incestuous text. Incest as an unconscious mode for the appropriation
of the daughter-female by the father-male: an apt screen for
justifying de$_{-facto}^{-feat}$ rape. Mother-son incest propounding
symbolic not factual castration. Symbol and carnal matter couple
here like systems where the daughter-woman is already expiating
the possible birth of a new being. To submit to the father (in
body) or in representation (brother, lover, husband) brings every
woman back to her illegitimacy. Her big belly. No waist, no
stature, daughter.

And act$_{ed\ upon}^{ually}$ however, if she wants to survive, a woman
must assert herself in reality and become recognized as symbolic
mother: incestuous in power but inaccessible sexually for reproduction. She then completely fills the space of desire and so can
appropriate for herself the work of the other. Strategic inversion:
this symbolic woman-mother has lost her womb. But preserves
the hues and stripes of her sex. Second mother, she can only be
the cruel stepmother. Strong but entrenched within a patriarchy.

Every thirty years a girl is born. Nobody knows whether she will
kill the womb and thus become the first and last legitimate
woman. So putting an end to His-tory. To fiction: *putting out the
last fantasy about women in heat and about beautiful schizo-
phrenics laying the discrete charms of steel along their wrists.*

Inside the matter of her womb. Lotus head. Inverted image, I burn its eyes. Time at the heart of language, maternal cell. At intervals, there's vibration. I am captivated from within, this body. From which I break out. Neither pyramid, nor castle, nor skyscraper. This body has the gender of its brain: feminine as in the beginning.

Nothing in the motion of her hand on her hair can be conquered except my beautiful eye, unstitched like a button, which looks at her. Hanging on her breast.

Into what can she want to initiate me. Patriarchal mothers able only to initiate their daughters to a man. There is no confidence between us. Sold-out, at a loss. Split in two, multiplied, in the gaze a crystalline lens unsure of the closeness or remoteness of others. To write about it would be a woman's eye resting on others, on things. To create her own locus of desire. To find her own place at a distance. So as not to wither up under each caress. So as not to knock the caress away.

She who is writing in the present between barbed wires remembers her past. Maybe they've been forced to cut *the current.* She goes through.

I open her mouth with my thumb and index finger. The struggle begins in silence. The search. I part her lips: 'monster's chops' or 'angel's lips'. I have to see for my own ends. She lets me do it, I don't threaten any part of her true identity yet. She's my m ther, she knows it and I am supposed to know it just as well. Her mouth like an essential and vital egg, ambiguous. In the beginning. AAAAA. My thumb masters the lower jaw. Her breath is in my eyes. To know all about her breath. About the food she feeds herself. My m ther drinks her beer. Swallows. I have my index finger on her gum as if to give her an order. But it's only an image. She bares her teeth. Invades me with her laugh. For an initial act: the transfer of powers. Clipped words that I must pass through in order to conquer the flowing words that fecundated her through the ear. Sharp words, full of gaps, about my m ther that I work on as if I were arming myself. She drinks her beer. Amazon. Her identity is not single. The power she confers on my thumb is very different; more than just going into my mouth as a surrogate. If I suck it must be my whole body. And open her mouth for her. Speak to me. 'No. Mummy is near, she's writing, my lu llay.'

The relationship with this woman is biological, material. Hand to hand. Body against body. Nourishment. She could have pulled me back by the digestive tube and swallowed her child out of murderous hunger. Cannibalism of survival. Materialism. But she could not. Materialism is only reached by the symbolic route. I haven't yet become her *child*. She is not yet my *mother*. Not a word separates us. Several years later I'll call her my mother. I've lost *Mommy*. That could become a book.

Every morning I am called Mommy. I get up. I kiss her and I get her breakfast ready. We separate for the day. Because I have to write this book. As if to rid ourselves of a symbolic relationship or to begin to execute it: daughter-mother lesbians. But we still haven't got our mutual autonomy. Her way is littered with objects she cannot reach. I open the refrigerator door. I open the drawers. I cook the food. My time is fragmented by these same objects. I am stuck to matter. Things are what I touch. I can neither dream them nor estimate their exchange value. Just like me, things are useful to keep me as well as the child alive. 'I polish them unceasingly like fine bones'.†

† Translator's note: Anne Hébert. 'The Thin Girl.' Trans. by Alan Brown.

The only product a mother can use as a medium of exchange is her child. Her only enterprise: 50% of the primary matter (ovum), gestation (the uterus as tool, instrument), production (giving birth), marketing (her labouring strength: arms, legs, bearing down). But she cannot exchange her product. Entering the economic system as subject, she must also pass into the symbolic system as subject. Stuck in matter and to her child, she has no access to it whatsoever. Stammer. Stutter. Mmmme mess.

Prostitute, she would have found takers and profit. Finished product (her body) which she offers in a very exacting code of exchange. It's the whole factory she sells. The joint. Real estate. She really can't be *apprehended*. She knows how to *make herself useful* in the symbolic domain, neighbouring, bordering. Which touches her.

In appropriating for himself the entire symbolic domain, that is to say a vision, man has made sure of his control by laying hands on all the modes of energetic production of the female body (brain, uterus, vagina, arms, legs, mouth, tongue). In so far as woman's body is fragmented, woman cannot broach the global vision of man.

I have murdered the womb and I am writing it.

Of all women, the mother (and ideally for the whole of patriarchal society, thus for all women) is the one who earns no profit *in actual fact*. Defeated. Each woman can profit only to the extent that she becomes symbolic mother. That is when she stopped bearing children. The milk sours. Mona Lisa smiles.

I write my daughter is sick. Fever. High. Anxiety: I have killed the womb. Caught in the whirlpool, the wave, the dread, the pallor, I write. What if I didn't stop for hours. Bodies die. Feverish.

light out: grey like a brain in the room. She and I are drinking our beer. She has just dyed her hair. Black. Would madness be as radical as tightening around us, I write my love.

...

you whistle in the kitchen. I hear the water moving around your hands and over your black blouse you are washing and my pink brassière.

...

A Sunday morning listening to Edith Piaf. All three of us dance. I am in their arms. We whisper sounds to each other in our ears and on our mouths. We dance very close together. Pressedhard. Nobody here wants to be lost. Matter and words. The moment but also because we are speaking. Carnal interrogatives. Imperatives like shoulders in the tango. Mommy is there, stranger like a different woman, close like a beginning. I am trying to make us afraid of nothing, not them, nor me, nor her.

My mother by abstention, write so I abstain from you. The fever has dropped.

It is while caressing the body of another woman over its entire living surface that she kills the mother, that the identical woman is born. A ghost who gives her vision, which version?

It is not the mother's body which decays but that of every woman who has not found words to look at the bruised womb: the body of the mother as extended fiction. Matter. Our mother's bodies displaced, inverted as if the womb were to be found in place of the brain. Domesticated symbol. Entering the heart of the subject matter properly speaking, become material-ist, in other words, to prepare one's capital on the maternal tomb. Ideological dead-end: word for word to escape the hand to hand, body against body. The biological mother isn't killed without a simultaneous explosion of fiction, ideology, utterance.

The dead mother laid out like a theoretical cloud above the mad eyes of Einstein's mother. (Mère) She covering (mer) sea like a perfect synthesis. Neo-realism.

Base of operations bankrupt: she can build a base on no one, she is her own saftey device. But sabotaged by the words of smother, bitter death. Unacceptable. The only thing admissible is the labouring body of the daughter mother. Since to go back up the current leads to the primal symmetry of the womb, that long blue line which on the body of the daughter mother stretches out already like an ideological current — you shall bear children in pain — you shall give birth quite naturally. Every distinction which already takes away her body and her senses (the very expression on her face) by force of words keeps her at the other end, exiled, brought forth from him, aborted like a woman. He took possession of the child as of a word in the dictionary.

Her mother's daughter. A finger between my two lips close, as they say, as the bark and the tree, bringing about the ellipsis daughter mother which makes the passing from one to the other without intermediary without interruption. Couple and generation at one and the same time. Instantaneity. Of death in its process. Blossoming: new cortex.

Before withdrawing. His-tory. She can only explode it, its passions, its parallels, its parameters. Bulging her belly one last time. For a girl.

To pass from one to the other. Which in itself eliminates all reproduction for the benefit of a single being. 'God is dead', the women pass from one to another through the very eye of the needle preparing the resistance. The final assault on the womb. Mutation. Uterus stitched up. 'Mother died today.'†

To experience bliss in the ultimate intercourse like two signifiers and metamorphose so mutually that they contain a single meaning, these women succeed in doing it.

In this region initiation between their mother's thighs makes sense to the daughters. Definite, these girls know then how to perform their own rite. They officiate. Blue words in the eyes. Nobody will infiltrate them, advance on them. Symbolic mothers, they have begun to spread. Nylon in hand. Since breasts will no longer smother anybody.

† Translator's note: Albert Camus. *The Outsider.* Trans. by Stuart Gilbert.

I am sitting on a bench in the park. My daughter is playing in the sand, right beside us. The other mothers who, we look at their children patiently. We don't speak a word to each other: what is there to exchange? A child. We could not do it. In silence we watch them disappear in the white bubble, the tear. At the sound of their cries. Fiction about us mothers, like great ostriches taking out little cookies and kleenex so that the children will stop burrowing in the sand to get away from us.

Here is the clan of patriarchal mothers. Devoted to men. Raising their young. Who have nothing to say. To exchange a domestic silence. Enclosed.

Placed one after the other in contradiction. My daughter is playing in the sand, right beside us. The other mothers. The silence here is unbearable. Everything gravitates about a senseless grammar. I killed the womb too soon, alone and primitive in a park with for my entire vision, between a child's legs, brushing against the smooth flesh, the inaccuracy ageless, deliberate steps, the trampled grass.

All this time that she remains in the story, in his-tory, she can earn her living only by disturbing the symbolic field. Modifying the first clause, the instrument of reproduction, her only tool. The dissolution of forms, like an end of the world played on the stage of the flat belly. Her uterus set beside her like a backpack. That presupposes a reorganization of her whole body, her means of moving about. She has room to pass in front of the mirror. A space to reflect her living body on the gleaming ribs of the man, who ... / she is silhouetted, potential touching two hemispheres at once like a callous body. Maternal matrix and materialist. She reorganizes her material: private and political life. An equation of life.

In peace time, in war time, she resorts to words.

About a woman's sex. Mythically covered by. Escorted away. 'There was an evening, there was a morning.' A story stretched out in the grass. Infernal coitus. Without mask, nor mask, without genitals, nor genitals, without woman, nor woman, nor words. Who could have withstood this stream of glowing embers around the anus, around the mouth. Like two cancerous deaths. Two theatres of men. The mother silhouetted between them. Writing. Embossed. Beside her posed like a girl, a woman.

To work myself into the grave over a body, to expiate all the symbols one by one, violence, like the stake, the witches, one by one. To have done with expiation. Inner torture. Madness. Among women we could liquidate madness, its fiction how it fascinates me, this power to excite me just like with another woman, there must be, this liquid in my spinal cord, an identity.

Like a large mark of tenacious lips on the clitoris, it moves, this historical orgasm, this one about the meeting of forces. Excitation through violence. Phantasm of the oppos-ite sex. The species, from murdered bodies.

a long time lo(u)nging our bodies two-gether to pass under cover of night. Mad and incompatible like two aborted heterosexuals who cannot penetrate each other. The scar must form. I put my mouth with your sex. Inner saliva. Eat and think as though there were no end.

The bodies of mothers entwined, in reality, it is also mine uneasy and enraptured by this heredity which takes shape inside the water drop, seaweed brushing eyelash. My form is no longer intact entwined with her body, but like a structure adorned for sexual bliss. Publicly fiction, publicly escapades, frescoes, multiple in the prism, the daughter mothers cavalierly public and fantastic stretching out their arms like sexual intercessions in the political pages of the daily paper. The bodies of mothers entwined, in reality, is a truly beautiful expression.

The State of Difference

Everything is possible, the worst seems probable. Enough circumspection! In a flash know the whole truth! there are breasts! ... Anarchy is on the rise, — I hope it will be worthy the name revolt.
COLETTE

Sunday: in my mother's arms, I am in a woman's arms and I am looking at my father. He looks at us. Tenderly. It's his day. My mother looks at me. I am touching my mother. Her body is obvious, I know her like a sensation. But to know him, I need my eyes, I must speak to him. He won't let himself be touched. He'll wait until I can speak before showing interest in me. Bigamous dog.

They are different: she and I touch each other. *He* speaks to me. I don't understand very well. I have to concentrate. I can't both keep the physical contact with my mother and listen to him at the same time. I try to understand him. To get a grasp on him. He's my father after all. He's existing. I must learn to speak. Word for word, like him. To reflect. If he pretends to understand me because he loves me his little girl, little joy, I will have won. We will have spoken once in a lifetime: that will be enough for me. If he doesn't consent, all my life I'll wait for that word from him. He'll speak on my behalf. A whole lifetime. No question of my mother coming to touch me when he is there.

The daughter has seen her father's sex as if in a dream. Fiction: reality comes out from her eyes.

So between him (his flesh his power) and me a distance: words. To have access to them. To move a body different from mine, a function different from the female, to be moved by the difference which works in me, like the words, spaced out, agitated lapsus. I have entered the book pinned down alive by this first struggle, my hand pushing back my mother's body, my mouth parted to organize myself like him, to speak *the truth,* to lay down the law. Under his eyes. Then to align myself at his side. But act$_{\text{ed upon,}}^{\text{ually}}$ stranger like a different sex.

Not another word. Silence. Muscular strength. The Law of the Muscle 'definitely she is somewhere between silence and shout' is established. As in the past he judges me and in point of fact lays the blame on me. And this time, I am alone: not in my mother's arms, without another woman bound by touch and voice. Skin dead with fear. Dead letter. A matching rag for each she-ape. Difference has taken over. Has established itself like him in my life. Surrounds me like a territory. His difference is transformed into *systematic* power. From this point he secures for himself control of the differences.

Modifying my function, I trans*form* myself. Work in the hollow of the belly: curetage. Making irregular, cataclysm of forms.

I chose to speak first about his look. Because this is where the perception of difference begins. In this way difference is confirmed and nourished. Science of looking: observation. Exact use of difference: control and mastery of that which is under observation, calling on the logic of specialization.

He lives in an ideological *laboratory,* apprehending formal and consequently functional differences. What he carries within him is moving before his eyes as a difference which he manages to isolate so as better to restrain it, to constrain himself. What he chooses to look at, he absolutely refuses to look like. Each new piece of information feeds the great collective computer. Comes back to him, as an individual, only after having completed its historical cycle. Only in the long term can he appropriate for himself the meaning of what he has observed: life. Or his son. In order to recoup (urgency the neurotic) a little of his expenditure, of his look, he will use the ideological road to stretch the evidence, trying to produce a factitious unanimity on the basis of differences.

To abolish the difference that he himself has chosen to accentuate, seeking to swallow her up *she weighs heavily inside like a mother.* Unbearable but urgently necessary in order to reproduce him. So she will be coded, legislated. Blood-stained.

Now. In planetary terms, my difference is no longer useful. It is no longer relevant, except where he still wishes to mark his own difference: a national population policy of arms. His difference includes me. Written into all the books. Advertized everywhere about and in me. Phallic architecture. Patriarchal daughters. Of my primary difference there remains only an ideological one (since I can no longer bear children). That is when the process itself forces me in turn to take up ideology. He is a symbol for me because now I am writing I can manipulate him. Daughter-mother lesbian, I write down the ultimate contradiction. Undermining from within his-tory in which I can now participate. The acid has begun to soak into the paper of the book.

The differences rise up like old cut-outs glued onto the paper of the book. Making the whole book expand. Ideological swellings. The race for symbols. Save yourself if you can with your own energy. Symmetry in the eye, stymied like a dialectic. Blinding it. This effect which gives our bodies derived meaning. Senses adrift. Memory of the difference: carcass or the interior fragile muscle. Full-fledged in fiction. Unity of connection — all this time that I have looked at my father, looking at us, my mother and me like a mythical statue, I knew that *the difference* would come from there: looking at him while thinking of what I could write on his tombstone. Like a work of art: calligraphic alphabet of my childhood. This childish de-sign, un-bosomed.

An unique identical woman. The difference with her and me is that we know the road backwards, from object to subject. The resemblance that brings us together with touch and the idea we have about ourselves. In *function* of ourselves: formal operation on which we concentrate our energy. In *function* of ourselves, women, can that make any sense; at the very least engender movement. Caught alive as if we had slipped into the breach we ourselves had opened. Immobilized and ardent at the same time. Will this book be the product of a fever or of a major exercise in survival. Twist of the hips which gets me out of the abyss. Hands red with ink scratching the earth above me, where the patriarchal daughters walk about on dry ground busy mimicking the freshly shaved faces of the cloudless morning. Maternal clowns, king's fools filles du roi. Obliging. All I can see is their ankles, chained, assembly line.

The difference is that I can't live deferred. To postpone the transformation, the synthesis of an unique identical woman. And it is this very difference that I seek on your body, different, of a woman with the same glance as mine. Identical with yours. Similar like a differential equation. Derivative of our functions. Point blank in the luminous spectrum. Projected one against the other as if in a polysemous dream.

What the eyes saw was the other. Not difference, but otherness. She was brought back to the dark cell, he brought back to power. Very quickly, the difference. Original/ reproduction. The senseless placing under guardianship. Dead pupil or the system of death as dialogue in order to reinvent life in words. To repeat to oneself white faced in front of the mirror: I am no longer *the same*.

A woman in front of the mirror looks for her identity. And sees there only an allusion. Illusion, metamorphosis: the gaze of the other. Obsession or juxtaposition of her bodies, mother's and woman's. No, she hasn't thrown her head back because of the bliss of orgasm. She was completely bowled over at the very idea that difference cut her in two.

The difference is what is left. The result of subtraction.

To consent to difference is to acknowledge structure, vital fact of every organism. However it is with a refusal of difference (acknowledged) that every ideological struggle starts.

That is when some meaning was displaced into the space of the body itself, its memory, its present. Fictitious and real it gravitated touching the unwonted white shapes of the sun.

From that it will be concluded that the entire body was concentrated within itself. Consented at noon, without a single mark in its vicinity.

At grips with reality — her difference — arches words let fly.

So difference brings us back into the private life of an organism bent on survival as well as bliss, rent even in its orgasmic function by the *idea* it organizes within itself like the secret happiness of a unified state in which the singular *body* has stopped living, where the body politic assures its living decomposition.

The shattering of difference like an entrance into fiction. An active bliss of rupture. At the same time my body opens. But a fissure and not the fragment. Opening into the density of matter. One day and the consciousness of a sharp explosion in the slit. Inside the opening all differences are excited since colour is sensation, from mauve to red, difference. Or while the body is being tattooed on the outside. But within my own difference I see clearly. Consistency: strictly one and the other. We cannot hide from ourselves the fictional character of the first A. discerning the hidden bond which frees the body.

From difference to difference: the interface. A space for fiction. Going back to the source, following the current and often short-circuiting, but in a line as though sliding on the inner surfaces. You become different inward to such an extent and so intensely that my memory is stirred up, double and gnawing to be filled. Like an effective scandal, the interminable fiction which always leads me back to the body of another woman. To conquer difference itself.

Five o'clock in the park, I rest my head on a shoulder as if on the trigger. There is some blue, Friday, today. This is a premeditated book.

In silence, I am dreaming of neuter, in front of the big linen press, opening the door on winter and woollens. Somewhere else entirely. Scenario of the smooth and soapy; in the kitchen drying the utensils we exchange between ourselves like money. Difference. The high stake of the coin. I speak to you. Who is trying to understand a pre-constructed, well known writing resonating in her ear. And yet the blending of the dishes and the words here said, here writ on the kitchen wall. You are looking for neuter and I for the beginning. But nothing stops, we are set down there, in our desires. Friction. But everyday life. Fullness. Fat. The one of us who will steal fire, sacrificing difference and identity for the essence, for gas. Little pile, weak nerves. To be swept in the kitchen. I assent to the difference, we'll lose a sex here. It will be entranced. And a white out in the memory. Just before I go to bed. Woman's writing. So be it, cachemire and nightmare. But you still touch me inside my mouth enough to make me assent to identity. Silk, ink or saliva. Free association. Perverse like an ongoing sensation of mothering. And wets posture and desire. Grating the salt at night on the surfaces, leaving there the mark of esoteric bitches. Plural women and without witness, nonetheless it is the uprising. With a single difference.

The difference: one breast. Amazonian or cancerous. Mother's daughter or patriarchal daughter.

Amputating oneself. Amputated. The one composing with science and knowledge: woman surgeon. The other woman: decomposed like a nude descending the staircase, a white bride. Invisible and mythical. The other: mythical or censured. Fiction of the unbearable, she comes into my memory and my words now, after the passage from the patriarchal daughter on whom I have never looked back, so much alike then, compelled now to look under her blouse, at her breast, my sister, how did it happen? Cancerous, schizophrenic. Beds. Stretched out and pinned down alive. I am looking at us face to face. You have stopped having children. The symptom in your body forced you into it. Writing it, I can only resist the symptom. Then to inscribe myself in the practice of a surgery sympathetic to our differences, effective and ridiculous like an ideology in tune with its historical situation, repressed within the limitations necessary for my survival as a woman unexpectedly arrived at a time when she can only kill the myth of her *the* woman who daily surf. Token.

So then, the other side, the difference: energy my own. A true fantasy which makes history outrageous and demented, which can only be generated by an unambiguous code. And also at the same time carries me away. Brings me back to myself as the sole entity that can make sense.

Hallucinate the difference, inner space, woman of interiors, stirred up in me with the very pain of giving birth. Caesarian. They would have permitted the other of the Rorschach on my belly, the perfect symmetry of the interior, in its contours positioned like the speakable geography of anxiety.

A reading, that is to say, following the lines of a branching anxiety with no other route than that of attracted eyes.

Exoticism of difference: exodus of the other and exile in the centre of the circle. Caught in the trap of confinement. Enclosed. And the more I consent to suffering, the greater the demand to watch me sickening like an overwhelming pornographic film showing the woman and man on the screen and the latter dealing out death defeat as life is taken at the very moment of filming. Murder. Cementing in this way the fissure, the breech between fantasy and reality, thus preventing even the circulation of all fiction. Putting an end to the social contract. News items. Diversion.

Erotic. Here I am in high martial art, at the mercy, pretending-resembling in agreement with the rules of his game; different and a stranger to the high stakes of conquest. Collapsed. Loser. He has his eyes everywhere on my body.

Take in hand the mastery of the symbolic. In no way assent to erotic (ideological) *argument*.

(ideological). We are entering a time when the logic of identity begins visibly: homoindividual. However, carried along or compelled by the idea we have of the future, we (wo)men flounder about feet and wrists bound in ideologies in passage, vital for individual equilibrium, necessary collectively like the biochemical requirements for a process. Motion: that is to say, the maintaining of the reproductive function of the body as well as ideological reproduction and production. Differences, suppose, struggle: and fiction filtering through the double inner wall at the same time, the self and its double, as the beach and the rock are almost always found facing each other on the banks of a river. The same water course. In the short run, stability of earth and movement of water. In the long run, landscape modified. A different shape.

Difference: these men and women on the two banks swim differently. And those from the beach have taken to sailing. On the rock, their initials, a buffalo, eagle, serpent, sheep, mother and all kinds of symbol. The echo. Reproduction in space. Head against the rock. Cave dwellers. To write: I am a woman is heavy with consequences.

Monday. Soapy water. It's been three days since I washed diapers. Or sheets, or a blouse; or myself. Tomorrow, I am menstruating.

Sensation of a difference. All smooth, all plump, this sex without pubic hair takes me back to childhood. Little girl gradual opening that my daughter recognizes with surprise as almost her own. Woman-daughter. We give birth shaved like a girl who has trafficked with the enemy. Nude hairless pubis, a bit of white whiter than a description of snow on the summit of a Japanese painting. Inside out slit. Hand curious to find itself a little girl again. Nervous tips of fingers. There, as in a flashing likeness, an endless fall through time and all the sensation of *the woman at olibos surprized by a man of letters.*

Had to act inversely to the letter and the voyeur: alone, as one writes, in the bath room, bending down the head and forehead, spreading the legs a little, *I am in the habit of touching myself,* but to see the difference in myself, finding the girl again with the eyes and the exact memory, this feeling of after school, among girls, agile commandoes, changing our marks on the monthly report.

Among girls, smooth like the edges of sleep; revived, women, the hair has grown again, refuse, more than one.

The only possible difference is a formal one. Any other difference can only be ideologically grounded. Formal being understood here as functional (sic: ideology being functional too. Reproduction versus reproduction.) Short circuit in the rational. Where does the private begin where does the political stop, the fictional, the real. Stale like bread in the throat of my body. The idea: embody. The idea of death has caused more deaths than death itself, connecting in this way to the idea of life.

My body still instinctively stretches toward. A (the one in the beginning) to reproduce itself. (Textually) there is no question of it. In any letter I AM STERILE.

Also, whoever does not agree to my sterility, to their own, are they consenting to their own death, slow demographic strangulation. If both are sterile, (wo)men, difference is abolished. I dantikal like two identical bodies, in an asexual future, indefinite like space, precise like a neuron. No longer the idea of our bodies but the energy of the body itself. State of the mutating difference. Sign of the moult: brain to the quick. The dialectic founded on difference will have been useful only for that, to take the grey diamond out of the case.

Act of the Eye

Act of the Eye

Moreover everything will have been tried so that the eye, at least the eye, is not destroyed by the fires of desire. LUCE IRIGARAY

and revive. The high stake. The empty motion of arms outstretched and waving. To take. Retreat. Momentum: hip total component of the primed body. As we come back to the garden: ink surprised in gestation. Rise over or the eyelid oh sun membrane of the smooth. To scrutinize as one invades and also as imprints. The surface, neither more nor less than the darting glance the feverish loss of the singular — I visit the men in the museum. This eye is caught in the palace of flesh. To evaluate. To lay hands on as in war with eyes staring alive. the torture of salt affirmed in the eye. Opens so suddenly the mouth to put into focus.

Violent Act of the Eye

I ask, if I shall never see you again and fix my eyes on that solidity, what form will our communication take? VIRGINIA WOOLF

She shuts her eyes concerned with herself alone. Urgent, inner trouble, I clutter the room with objects and clothes *the yellow lace* like an hypothesis. The act of the eye prepares certainties. Shocks shockingly in free fall. She opens her eyes, form of perspective *for what purpose have I looked at*; the nature of the look when words are not so certain that the value is value at all costs. It would be enough to enlarge the pupil to the extreme of excitation so that blind an instant it may be bliss or the silence. Am I myself caught fictive moistening the white globe. The violent act of the eye makes me resist. But confused right from the first snow.

The Violent Act of the Eye On

I used to look at my bed. My shits had been hidden under the mattress, the hard flock mattress on the black iron bedstead. That bed had housed my shit. MARY BARNES

To constrain myself or about the contraction of writing it. Images rubbed one against the other. Retina accommodating me: this morning it rained. How grey weather voids meaning and everything in the vicinity. Tearfully, she moans beginning with an act that she assumes or summarizes in a chink of the eye with the clear vision of a frog on the edge of a pool. Says to herself that she has looked so well that she is no longer able to. To finish her sentence. White like an influx passing through her. Vengeance to the point of rolling the eye or of a delirium to pull to pieces. Under observation.

The Act of the Eye on Purple

Some lesbian lovers have seen their eye become the eye of their lover in the distance. MONIQUE WITTIG, SANDE ZEIG

As if to broach the vertigo, the smooth version of the shoulders of loving women's bodies or to find oneself there at the vital risk of lucidity women enlaced wonderful and close like a music. This evening, I run over and over in my head the foam and my mouth so that both shared in nourishing the meaning we find there stronger than the wind the sensation of bees, exhorting us into a garden. Slowly it entered through the eye, a serum, vital from one to the other. Women perturbed, new contingency, in a cycle to break through matters only when it is a question of our dilating atom or tulip glass. Free fall toward the meadow.

The Violent Act of the Eye on Enamoured Purple

— nothing but the beak and the eye and what is said about
them. CLAIRE LEJEUNE

To be sure, death prowls in their eye making them blanch like
bald women looking for a retreat. What did they dream about in
each of their tremors and executions. The erection of the City,
ghost town. The war of the sexes toys with her, swoops down on
her like a heart attack. The violent act of the eye on enamoured
purple articulates its system. Av(o)id. Who would have dreamed
that the erotic would be used to publish the deluxe paper for
tracing the portrait of a man penis in the mouth of a two-year-old
girl. Or an engorged woman. Or a burned-out girl. Or an
accosted woman. Or a famous girl so famous that she was
intern(aliz)ed and at everybody's service. Eye for eye. Blackout.

The Act of the Eye on Enamoured Purple In —

I looked with chameleon eyes upon the changing face of the world, looked with anonymous eyes upon my incomplete self. ANAIS NIN

Without delaying inform oneself like a beautiful prolonged truce we have strayed from our field, allured alive. To discern oneself: the visual distance makes the difference in content when close up makes the abstraction, if one looks for it. Then the morning, very early, when I turn over with the breasts very near and the unsure arms of curled up animals, the girl comes to stretch out between us women because her dream tells about our flanks about us like a murmur the only one from top to bottom of the house. The girl with us between the fine sheets is not conventional. Early risers.

The Violent Act of the Eye on Enamoured Purple Infiltrates

The power of second sight is the most natural thing. FLORA TRISTAN

Everything is so double that no exchange manages to clarify to what it belongs. Aphrodisiac or *treaty*. Inside to expose myself as if to writing to the lively violence of the waters and the blank weapons. Infiltrating until oblivion, origin. Frantic eye decked with diamonds. My constraint is in the look *from this angle*, I fear the sensation issues forth from me just as one feels an attraction toward. A connection with. Filtering the perspective: they say the fog lifts but who sows panic. Round out the eye. And contract a then so suggestive body. With my other eye indicating the scalp and head of hair but on the retina. Images as though to dissimulate the cipher of intentions. Numerous, about action.

The Violent Act of the Eye on Enamoured Purple Infiltrates Enraptured

The scandal is impressed forever on the depths of my
retina. HÉLÈNE OUVRARD

(Drink shuts the mouths up again verging on) the inside, dilates. The women snort basted together like wicks. Licks the lip (when she drinks coffee) unwound in her eye-lashes. Looks perfectly straight ahead but it might be said diffuse. They open the eye both certain and vulnerable: moist crystalline totally real in this way to see from near or far (the street more cities and the city) rubbing their gums to be to speak the inverse of the orifices (pouring themselves well versed another cup of coffee). Fundamentally.

The Violent Act of the Eye on Enamoured Purple Infiltrates Enraptured Unfolding

I keep a close watch on myself. I keep an eye on myself. FRANCE THÉORÊT

Here falls in love with and to struggle with myself all in motion as in an ancient technique of desiring from without the body to apprehend the other body, its knowledge and its experience. The imposture of wanting to live on waters and on sweat in the very posture of desire on the shoulder or near the loins or facing the other's mouth to conquer the multiple lives ever being deployed to adapt oneself so as not to die in cold or in heat alike. Nervous, going right up to the cortex. Regulating my sleep and waking. Siamese emerging in the double position or the meeting of eyes in a chemical joy just as slowly accessible, alpha enduring, some other forms.

The Violent Act of the Eye on Enamoured Purple Infiltrates Enraptured Unfolding *Her*

and we would only come out of the eye to eat HUGUETTE GAULIN

Her fall is drowned here or her private form beyond parentheses, this one, which caused them to be born being dubbed with prohibitions by extension but the passage the fiction amplifying the eye's chant. From to which body do you belong, confused territory, essential woman, so that I may be intact at my coming forth from the eye as if giving the reading back to my own, the strangeness is in order to circumscribe the tournament of lips a presentiment of forms placed on the margin or so transparent as to be unanimous in deciphering the relationship just as in identifying sounds a bit in nature.

Figure

The figure is real like a political intent to subject her to the plural before our eyes, or, singularly, to power. The realistic figure is thus the most submissive there is. Quite simply, she agrees. She can be reduced then to the general (to the house) by using the singular: woman or image of milk women, *lait figures.* So the figure turns, two-faced, accelerates, bores into the eyes, the incidents, again, in a final struggle against blindness: apprehend her. Now the figure is in motion. At full speed the figure is unrecognizable. Intense unreadable. Sequence. The figure is migratory.

Figuration

She breaks the contract binding her to figuration. In the theatre of the past full of countless nostalgias, she alone, along with all women, creates the entire body of impressions. Not mythical like the double bodies sacrificed during *scenes*. The body-shock or nerve-impulse that prepares for action without alibi, a body where one is alone, in this case. The body of one cut off from retreat. Girl's body manifested in the precise sense of conflict. Arch, rising delirium: did anybody notice that during the scene passion riddled the eyes like the insertion of a woman into an inverted context. That's because in her interpretation of figuration, of apparent form, visibly, she modified the dream.

Disfigure

Tracks to de-face or make unrecognizable. Because after remoteness or open-mouthed privation how can you undertake a word-by-word within the figure: meaning: *in the state of nature* civilized like a deviation or multiple marginals. In transforming laughter. It must be written down that hate cannot be written or death like a political anxiety: in children's stories, the ogre's life explodes breaking food, bodies into pieces; girls come out of the houses as from the context. In the forest, heads will be bounced on pensive knees. The abyss or into the gulf thrusting them aside. Distancing as for a fiction.

Geometrical

Issue of gorges circles sphere spirals: butterflies or the result of emotion. The figures tumble about: on the surfaces, refracted, intimate pauses. To attempt the delay of space without line without writing only the war of limbs of frantic arms of tepid hands. Projected: an illusion of gills of water of tresses — eyes become feeble in space intentionally, from acting with fresh perception. Let them close like watertight mouths in an optical slow motion of premonitory cats on a full mid-season day.

On Intention

She has multiple intentions but one of them is always much too hidden: her body like a paradox of matter *seeing that* she has patiently waited ovaries of several intensive centuries of intension-survival at the frontier of the eyes, day after day the tracing. The beginning again. The rings circling the eyes get bigger. So in contrast the figure (or like a reflex) designates a new configuration fit for inflecting the common meaning. In a hurry to attain a dimension other than symbolic. But the figure reaches its fullness: steps over the taboo or the transient buttocks of a male. Beyond terrorism. The other passions brave the trajectory, pressed in their materiality, that other form of fold.

Taken Figuratively

In the flow to deliver meaning or to utter with concision – who is she depicted manners and propitious as presumed victim, who is she, knows it, ellipsis or sometimes when she bears, that displaces the shadow and the effect of long nights begins to make itself felt on the surface or intensely. Her thirst like playing tricks on the desert, inevitably: grasping the figurative and proliferation. When the profiles move getting ready to speak. It's the shivering or perhaps the rustling of paper. Is an apple on the work bench enough to make sense? Or to turn the stomach?

The Figurine

Hunted to earth but in my hand can she stop my death what is she doing on my grave (on horseback) ochre terra cotta, the stone, her breasts where's her mouth then let her put new life into the disintegrated part of the body. There you have millennium and silence. Would have been put in a museum, large-hipped Venus. Sometimes any intention whatsoever … but slowing down often makes me converge on the fountainhead. It's her belly. How fruitful she was with her castrating sex. The figurine, it's through the eyes, from time to time the mouth, that a distant reign, in my hand, salt, breast.

Has Figure(d)

Say what: reality — collar halter stall — we've seen them, tied down, bound daily or white bitches in the morning. Reality doesn't exist. Go see five o'clock come. It doesn't exist, it's still light. It's somewhere else. Don't talk to me about reality. Nor appearance. It remains to be foreseen. But to have access. Or to begin again. That doesn't exist. Where is your Utopia in the drawer in Mummy's room? Reality, that's life and it's an illusion. White arms in the snow. For sure that doesn't exist. Long before I tremble. Great fear that it doesn't exist. Or else on the sea the wave inside the hollows, softness. In fact all it is is the intense body far from his eyes well positioned *to know*. That has nothing to do with it. But know the alert figure, stature and history. In hereality.

Prefigure

To support muscle like a business, domestic. Agitated figure, of arms of fragments of vaginas within her always to be changed into bread or breast. Fictive that she be ideal because *I have a terrible time grasping* it's filled with junk like an attic. Shifting so that her body coincides with a few familiar sentences. The symptoms went away to her mo(u)rning mate oppressing him. In fact, she feels better without allergy. The figure is really a girl watching her childhoods, supposed to be a woman, but *in fact,* a girl. Always: overcome what obstructs the synthesis. About her passing through her own fiction, *ourle hurle houache illico,* hem howl wake then and there.

Free Figure

Constrained, remember: there is a clandestine space where every law is subordinate to the imaginary or if infiltrating it like a reality they make them rescind themselves. Cloudy water in appearance but interior tissues knowing the only way to go. All in all, it's a question of practice. The slope of that other passion. The same. Or it could be said when imagination catches fire, it ends up a fuse and political. One fecund and suffering trajectory of the body. One last ghostly vision in reality. No belly, no breast with no head lying attached to it, to remember.

The Vegetation

lies, sum up and I digress. The day after the seventh day, returned alive into the enigma. Tissues everywhere covering over the skin. And characters. Animals having learned from need to slip into what dimension. To rise up. Inert matter is the debate: slow to utter my other form as the word magically disperses rot. Meat, muscles. Here lies the repressed the evil silence old century and furrowed splendour. What is there to predict throughout the course of history? Nosferatu The Corriveau the thousand and one infusions at night before going to sleep the fear or the outrage ravaging the excess of silence and so many linings explodes best within

*

I was matter it's the vigil over the body. The other body on purpose, taken in its most unusual proximity. Some of its actions, one function, *the day before her menstruation, she was seen heading into the fields.* But in the city, that other body stirs pendulum oscillated wild from the head, from the erasure on each yes snatched and word.

Matter has always begun to move alone or was it in equation.

sap rising a stage over the entire expanse memory bush(y) cry lacerated chin tooth of dispersion the leafy animals which have come have not sought an alibi – but full skull mythical traces and trap high the cage above the void. Production against nature is incumbent in every condition or when it is said of me 'so natural', I remake myself.

*

The night is dyed with beautiful dreams but here when birds pass over: machine reverse: they go along the nerve disintegrate it until it must spear a black maternal picture and its entrails in flight. Would she have to harden herself so that she wouldn't dream of it any more. I see her coming. There will be a reconciliation somewhere: her tools my matter. But the hand we both have becomes animated all over, to cut into the stone.

*

Where it is seen that circulating here, everything can be put to work, the twisting of the lips, the taste of the baby for we too were cannibals and hairy on our breasts. As soft as thoughtful.

verse, tapeworm or Oedipal complex. To see the buying back of faeces as a product which later it will be advisable to exchange for words or when anger unbalances casting the evil spell, the forbidden manuscript. The buying back of the text in its child's mirror, there's still too much consciousness in this vegetation. Rain. Spittle. We look at ourselves: milk malice shining *the result of being in the world*. Before that towards me but with the eyes, but I want your immensity and warmth of body you must know our energies in a different way than in your belly but with the eyes. Asexu( ) or maybe invariable.

*

But then we will be thrown onto the street for *having* put into our heads another multiple-headed destiny. An aquatic synthesis or for deluge water colour and fish, soft water spine. Swim back up the political stream following closely *I to act hallucinate take my hand for a fan* to spread all out I want to be able to circulate freely. It's inside the dream or instinctively if I crouch down to think about it. The fog in the early morning my exaltation is well known. A few wants in the snow. The day begins. A long time ago. Fissure.

To tame and radically like an enigma for life. Femished or illusion on the shore. She will have raisedherhandonherbody beautiful scintillating. Image 's(h)ea of the bony marrow', the brain adrift fish serpent my female ancestor and mother-goddess everywhere in my neck enthusiastically. Enraptured that obscure, fast-flying and gusty pass by folded wrinkles near my eye. Watching the others come. The trajectory. Watch out for the heel. In the grass I'll have tried either the moon her hip or the whole weight of his body pressing on her trachea.

*

The look disintegrates slow premonition. How the strident voice aerial legs of yet other women and the music in one more night the dance. Relishes galvanized in the dawn desire rushing rushed the slope of the belly in the forgotten detail of the tympanum the words have seen her white.

The time it takes to utter is plausible: the other to devour or in the peril agitatedly. There is consistency in wanting all orgasmic bliss clandestine even though it might happen openly.

in the body but who hurts it in the belly. There is nothing to be spared. We have spent a long time winning the heart of the monster the body exuberant territory. The tracing: mutilations, slice. Anatomy. Now the body is no longer the body but the terrifying anecdote which feeds the ${grey \atop tank}$ed body.

＊

visually in the phantasm it is the shadow and irony the trace why in the eye the slice of life, its confines.

＊

maybe of death. There is an I only when the tear. And food. No limb but cavity. An activity in the duration, the precisely internal expanse moving about like a membrane.

under ground and in the hair with the hands the tongue diagonal cut: energies branch out to inaugurate in the vegetation. These real plans there's an inclination to want to overthrow an order *to offer myself to the first one I haven't spoken at all because he had women's hands a hand to hand fight believed to be feminine leaning myself against the murmur, wall of breath, embracing me* — instantaneity — I'll not write twice twice this discomfort of breasts slowly uncovered at auction but especially the nipple.

*

slowly closed up again. Words and mirrors to repeat me with a result but tenderness. A text. As if obliged to coincide in my eyes. In my mouth, before my eyes it makes me think of paper it's written just the same it has a woman's body in my eyes, the subject.

If I have entered into the vegetation it is in order to bring into view there not the repressed but the displayed. Pressed down played out the same, grass. Like an echo. What was not foreseen at all from the conditioning: the species agitating in the abyss and sprouting ever a bit more discomfort under each vertebra so that water adapts itself because audacities are part of the process of all mutation, among secret inclinations, the most inflaming. In the eardrum, there was always the same effect: water wave. Let them believe in energy, I was with some women then.

*

Because it is the possible acts which are most difficult to accomplish, there is some risk of being in complicity *blue fears their trace trance in the storm* systematically some forms to be on the watch shoulder sex character thunderstorm s(ea)our-mothertune. Such an incident in the depths of the eye aggravates improvisations.

In the centre of the grasses dream of the letter in the beginning 'fluvial dog-toothed women. They are white and very fine' as among the female monsters described (voured); this part of me sprouts deliberately renews the stages (the eyelid its thickness) or the sense which revives by means of fire of root and salt. All appearances in peril: does the verb of action really circulate in the green fauna or must a garden a square park dice game assure technique its true luxury for the eye. Its off shoots.

*

strident stria strix† night flocks with dense tufts, with the special effects that loss of reality produces. Only the past or previous states have an interior but in the slowness of arms in the clearing the displaying of intense animation — I want to run the risk of the deliberated belly as though with shores and rages within do you want the posture to sound fantastical in your ears.

† strix zool. term for night birds of prey, stryga — female and dog vampires.

Where I am so they say there are no words the underground face hasn't a word unless in the distance and echo: montage of sound or safety device. A tendency to be inverted in-pulsion. 'See on the other hand' like the double perspective in your eyes because in speculating on the repressed the tightly packed I deploy without even a horizon. Fiction in which almost nothing of the body in its evolution escapes. Mid-way skidding unsteady ankle.

*

None of what appears in front of me could be nourished or even in a state of being if I didn't break in from the margin where *I have plunged within myself* not the woman but the little girl the mutilated girl resisting *the* woman. Everything (makes) *this body* evolving agitatedly in space, whose feet never rest because she has no shadow is it. Now battle seasoned like synovial humours, melancholy, salivating. weaves the a the acme the ancient('s) course *only a murder out of nerve short of ink* av(o)id for words she mistrusts washes away the lips lapsus speaks ironically or cries it to death so that av(o)id to find the others there ferreting about everywhere with: displacement of the earth and re(in)volution of the matrix. The knowing hand knows how at a distance to produce and will the belly *in any case,* the silence of the valleys must be dilapidated without discretion.

*

motif in mind to divert every reply you day dream in the crystal but to reassure no one — that assassin rushing sweating with ardour as though mingling with the crowd inside. she was soft hairy with desire during *physical contact.* Wherever the eyes come from, I get pigheaded and proceed *civilized among the vegetation.* At the height of summer, while we were making great gestures fierce and insistent. A temptation the story and secretion.

well versed in (the) matter, hands; the ones given in marriage. This evening when the shapes rise up or when to disclose the umbilicus, groping hands the result of suffering, the absorbed women come out of matter. Know that each tool gives rise to differences. Without tools, their hands can only be knowing and skilful which is taken for gentleness. Their fists when they close up like their mouth, in silence. Done for webbed to change swaddling bands. Synthesis of ever peripheral hands. Premonitory this time: some tools on the table. Hands on.

*

at the quick in the conflict at the speed of wrists breasts smell of battle of fear knowing that around the clover here lies how in reality the combat makes the whiteness of the displayed nerve appear. It is possible that all this is true, the flesh put away until later and the body accessible for others. With respect to life, all along this brief book s(our) mother like fear or all about batting eyelashes, walking woman†

† In the feminine, *promeneuse* evokes Rousseau's 'Confessions d'un promeneur solitaire.'

Take risks inside, with the finger in the throat to make the sleeping muse vomit. To see it come up. At the same time, myths abounding, fauna swaying. The hollow of the breasts. The girl looks at the women far away: mirage. To reach that point in person, contemporary.

*

fiction forms foliage tea in a whisper. *To reach that point,* seizure, is it possible or really true the corpse or the body and the rape, the foetus, ready to defy reality when everything turns like a confession, fluid, ready to make the law, she's astounded, in view of which

*

for other compatible reasons, move a little to see whether the body continues to exist actually or just on occasion. Mime, it's torrid.

ravarage in the neck to the life blood the throbbing obsession that to dream is it to scent out 'whether I am orgasmic', an intersection of the text, its essential fragment, the inscription of the miser but I who seek in *the spending* the orgasmic totality of desiring fragments. The $^{f}_{d}e^{e}_{a}$d. At regular intervals, intractable floating somewhere, all in all it's exciting

*

the approach on foot so as to get a direct reply from my mouth will you say or versatile miscible tongue with noise salt skin to convince you before the patriarchy that the mouth m$^{oves}_{oults}$ again with an I — that I am becoming lettered is civilized but body identical to the sea pink girls sirens behind closed doors no exit. To begin her story 'this girl's reason(able)'

The Fictions

PRIVATE FICTION

private fiction or the concerned body how was the flesh fictive has she been able to begin a staging, I began to describe the incomprehensible effects of child's flesh in my eye, taken to my bed (April 25th) partly at night but dawn soon, legs red, they put on gloves while I was sleeping, to open me up. The black haired girl, under glass, stirs, like a beginning: the flesh is going to become civilized.

*

her body, while he looks at her (May 15th) unreeling all the cylinders in front of her, concretely he rapes her, *words say it* for him *that quite instinctively*: assault. It happened during the day. She represents in his eyes/brutally in the flesh. But she can no longer bear to be so encumbered. It happened, on a working day. Began to hit out, knife in his ribs.

breath flowers organ orange everything slides into the mouth, slice of life, this flesh has stopped moving, ultimately is it fiction that a corpse or *the body of* (June 5th) fixed in purple death what a difference.

*

fiction of the next day is it true that the bodies of mothers entwined last night, before the children were put to bed (October 7th) has distinguished in the dark the unquestionable project of reviving, of intercepting signs their meaning on the bellies like mouths for navels very alive. The children are not sleeping yet, it is present, in memory, that they ask where are the pyjamas. And that the body of the intertwined mothers makes no reply.

POLITICAL FICTION

To depart from his-tory, the imagination a fulgent proximity among rebels that will encircle this event from inside: rite of passage. Unequivocally, the backbone and its slopes must be crossed, the body and any commerce it undertakes. Certain aspects of reality that put us in *this state* when vision becomes theoretical, an intuition which being inner admits lucidity as a technique for contemplation. Sweet machination it is to escape the shattering glasses of history, the hunters of embers *at a particular moment in a life*. A specific worry about vitality that makes me identify reality I only barely remember. Attentive to the moment when action may unexpectedly happen. From fictive to political. Rubbing against quotation. But noisily, under the epidermis, the temptation of rising up a barbarian.

when I say body, all the tensions, the secretions without intermission exposed in its concreteness, excess of ivy and political partition. Real or exquisite survival all at once embraces but hunger. Profusion of limbs in the head when the body returns to the house to cook its egg there. When I say body I expose myself, energy. Behind others' backs some signs completely broken by the wind parcelled, women's muscle, the nerve is the tongue that shines makes reread *I am succinct to bring the paradox to a head.* May the imaginary be a place where the code of the species is preserved at its best, that strange simplicity basically required to tackle the subject. All convention subjugated, it's delirious to approach matter like a conversation dispersing the institution. Or the person who would tell the narrative of a smile would reveal very intimate drama with no murderer, a geographical tension that has no thighs. So cunning. I must not die in the blue of the hunted-down finger-nail. In polishing an egg for myself against the heavy muscle of a male very heavy with the fallout of his learning cavity, auroral animal (to the extent to which the gap between fiction and theory is reduced, the ideological field is eaten up) the wound. Then from guts bullets jet out. Imagine. Tremble deservedly in the spring, serene premature: tomb and verdict. Don't think that death comes because of her or else you only reconstitute her. Then the dexterity of amazons breaking their arrows on *the white page* will be evoked chemistry offers its denizens nothing but breath oblivion the fleeting moment but it launches her mother's daughter for once into the verbose spectacle leaning on the wall the disordered face of grasses the hands' anxiety: manufacture of every body knowingly — truce, the ruts, dense is the urgency. Politically — . But reality from the lungs, there is only one image to bring it to a conclusion: summer, during the hours of heat, I am naked only to the storm, heavy with appetite. Successively in the multiple forms of a fiction, knowing suddenly only a process in slow motion where nobody wins except in the beginning, in the watchfulness into the blank this energy equilibrium, gifted with tenderness in the evolution. In the city, the traces, leave behind the high stakes, nicole, without erasure of fiction in front of our eyes, it is the eyelashes which during the pact serve to light up the night the whiteness that happens to come from our flesh, from the staring eye of girls without remorse. Unequivocally passing through the city, the City and all allusion to business. I am referring to childhood, to darkness overturned after the manner of the belly

I must carefully formulate the little experiment of frowning during the tremor I awake in myself the collective region, the costumes, only *the dramatic text* avalanche of scales, must be vested with improvisations around the life of the girls perforce taking closely after adults. Knowing nothing about it except the bloody flow. I am left with the foam or the merry-go-round of forms or to cry over one's self as though to establish an act in this sort of immobility when overwhelmed with an intention so subjectively, a word, the sheaf.

to anticipate that the political feat tactile tactical *in any case* it's preferable to apprehend the liaison with the very concrete bodies outside conventions, converging substances. Fiction retorts. I often feel this way: jaw gaping open around the brain, my limbs heavy with flesh.

Analysis: so that for me lips are represented as a motivation to follow mouths replete with affinities. In that way, I am working so that the convulsive habit of initiating girls to the male as in a contemporary practice of lobotomy will be lost. I want to see *in fact* the form of women organizing in the trajectory of the species.

Editor for the Press: Frank Davey
Typeset in Garamond and printed in Canada

For a list of other books,
write for our catalogue
or call us at (416) 979-2217.

The Coach House Press
401 (rear) Huron Street
Toronto, Canada M 5 S 2 G 5